A Bluestocking Guide

Political Philosophies

by

Jane A. Williams

based on Richard J. Maybury's book
ARE YOU LIBERAL? CONSERVATIVE? OR CONFUSED?

published by
Bluestocking Press

web site: www.BluestockingPress.com
Phone 800-959-8586

Printed and bound in the United States of America.
Cover Illustration by Bob O'Hara, Georgetown, CA
Cover design by Brian C. Williams, El Dorado, CA
Edited by Kathryn Daniels

ISBN-13:   978-0-942617-47-4 (soft cover : alk. paper)
ISBN-10:   0-942617-47-9 (soft cover : alk. paper)

Printed by McNaughton & Gunn, Inc.
Saline, MI USA   (January 2010)

Published by Bluestocking Press
P.O. Box 1014, Placerville, CA 95667-1014
web site: www.BluestockingPress.com

Quantity Discounts Available

Books published by Bluestocking Press are available at special quantity discounts for bulk purchases to individuals, businesses, schools, libraries, and associations, to be distributed as gifts, premiums, or as fund raisers.

For terms and discount schedule contact:

Special Sales Department
Bluestocking Press
Phone: 800-959-8586
email: CustomerService@BluestockingPress.com
web site: www.BluestockingPress.com

Specify how books are to be distributed: for classrooms, or as gifts, premiums, fund raisers — or to be resold.

Contents

Chapter Title	Questions	Answers

How to Use This Guide

Bluestocking Guides are designed to reinforce and enhance a student's understanding of the subject presented in the primer. The subject for this study guide is political philosophies. The primer is ARE YOU LIBERAL? CONSERVATIVE? OR CONFUSED? by Richard J. Maybury.

Given the wide range of age and ability levels of individuals who read ARE YOU LIBERAL? CONSERVATIVE? OR CONFUSED?, it is suggested that students complete the exercises in this study guide that are most age-appropriate or ability-appropriate for them.

Assignment of Exercises

While all given questions and assignments are designed to enhance the student's understanding and retention of the subject matter presented in the primer, it is by no means mandatory that each student complete every exercise in this study guide. This study guide is designed for flexibility based on a student's age, as well as a student's interest in the material presented.

It is strongly suggested that each student complete the Comprehension Exercises, but instructors can preview and then select the Application Exercises, Films to View, and Suggested Books to Read that they wish the student to complete, based on: course time available, student's interest, and/or student's age (some films/books might not be age appropriate — the student might be too young, too old, or the content too advanced for a younger student). Also, depending on the age and interest level of a student, one student might spend weeks on a research assignment, whereas another student might spend a few hours or days.

Suggested Time Frame For Study

This study guide is organized to allow the instructor flexibility in designing the ideal course of study. Therefore, there is no "right" or "wrong" time frame for covering the material; the instructor should tailor the study of the primer and study guide to the student's unique school schedule, learning style, and age. For example, younger students may only complete comprehension exercises, whereas older students may complete additional application exercises, suggested readings, and films.

An easy-to-apply rule of thumb for determining length of study is to divide the number of chapters in a primer by the number of weeks the instructor plans to study the subject/book.

Ideally, the student should read a chapter from the primer and then immediately answer the corresponding questions in the study guide. Chapter length varies, so sometimes a student may be able to read more than one chapter and complete the corresponding questions/exercises in a day. Some instructors may choose to complete the primer in a few short weeks in which case multiple chapters per day will need to be covered. Others may plan to study the primer over an entire semester, so only a few chapters per week will be assigned. The key is to move quickly enough that the student is engaged with learning and also able to absorb all concepts fully. The student's performance on end-of-chapter Questions and Assignments should be a good indication of this.

The time frame for completing application exercises (Discussion/Essay/Assignment/Research) is also subject to the instructor's discretion. Most discussions can take place immediately after reading the chapter. However, students may need a day or two to complete an essay, and some assignments will take outside research requiring additional time. It is best for the instructor to preview the application exercises (Discussion/Essay/Assignment/Research) and assign the student a "due date" based upon the student's cognitive abilities and available course schedule.

Comprehension Exercises

Comprehension Exercises test the degree to which the student understands and retains the information presented in each chapter. In this study guide Comprehension Exercises include: 1) Define, 2) True/False, and 3) Short Answer/Fill-In. Students are encouraged to answer all exercises in complete sentences. The information needed to complete these exercises can usually be found in the given chapter of the primer. Answers will be found in the answer section of this Study Guide.

Define

The student should define the given term based on Richard Maybury's definition provided in the given chapter or glossary (*not* a standard dictionary definition). This is essential. As Richard Maybury says, "Fuzzy language causes fuzzy thinking." For any discussion or explanation to be clearly understood, one must first understand the intended definition of words as used by the author. Confusion and disagreement can occur because the student does not understand the author's intended definition of a word. To reinforce this point, have a student look up the word "law" in an unabridged Webster's dictionary. The student should find a number of definitions following the word "law." Again, unless one agrees on the definition intended for the discussion or study at hand, misunderstanding or "fuzzy thinking" can result.

True/False

For True/False exercises, if the student believes the statement is correct, the student should simply write "True" as the answer. If the student believes the statement is *not* true, the student should write "False." If the student answers the question "False," the student should be sure to state why the statement is *not* true or rewrite the false statement to make it true. In the answer section of this study guide, statements that are "False" are so noted and have been rewritten to make them true.

Short Answer/Fill In

The student should answer Short Answer/Fill In questions based upon knowledge gained from studying the given chapter. Unless the student is asked to use his/her own opinion or knowledge, the answer should be based upon Richard Maybury's statements. Generally, Short Answer/Fill In Questions are selected verbatim from the given chapter.

Application Exercises

With few exceptions, Application Exercises ask the student to apply the knowledge and ideas he/she has gained from a given chapter to "real world" situations. In many cases, these assignments are designed to help the student personalize the information just learned so that the student can better retain and apply the knowledge. In this study guide application exercises include: 1) Discussion, 2) Essay, 3) Assignment, and 4) For Further Research. In the majority of instances, answers to Application Exercises will vary based upon the student's own experiences. Application Exercises are designed to encourage informal discussions among students and instructors, and/or to stimulate students to critically evaluate the scenario. However, the instructor may ask the student to write answers (in essay format, outline, etc.) if a more formal/structure approach is desired.

For Further Reading or To View

The books and films mentioned in For Further Reading and To View are designed to expand students' understanding of concepts presented in the related chapter. No written or verbal reports on the books/movies are usually required, however, students and instructors are encouraged to discuss the ideas presented. Thus, Suggestions for Further Reading/Viewing usually have no set answers and, therefore, may not appear in the "Answer" section. (The instructor may choose to assign a book/movie report of his/her own construction if he/she desires.)

How to Grade Assignments

Define, True/False, Short Answer/Fill-In

To determine the percentage of correct answers, divide the total number of correct answers by the total number of questions. If, for example, a chapter section has two Define questions, one True/False question, and seven Short Answer/Fill-In questions, and the student has answered correctly eight of these questions, the student will have answered 80% of the questions correctly.

$$8 \div 10 = .80 \text{ (or 80%)}$$

Number of Correct Answers ÷ Number of Total Questions
= Percentage of Questions Answered Correctly

In "Grade" equivalents, percentage scores generally range as follows:

90 - 100%	=	A
80 - 89.9%	=	B
70 - 79.9%	=	C
60 - 69.9%	=	D
less than 60%	=	F

In general, a student earning an "A" has demonstrated excellent understanding of the subject matter; a student earning a "B" has demonstrated good understanding of the subject matter; a student earning a "C" has demonstrated sufficient understanding of the subject matter; and a student earning a "D" or "F" would benefit from reviewing the subject matter to strengthen his/her understanding of the topic at hand.

In determining whether a student has provided a "right" or "wrong" answer to a question, the instructor should compare the student's answers with the answers provided in this guide. True/False, Fill-In, and Define questions/answers are straightforward. Short Answer questions/answers are also generally straightforward; on some longer answers the student's wording may vary slightly from the answer provided in this study guide, but the student should receive full credit if the *content* of his/her answer is correct. When in doubt, it is recommended that the instructor refer back to the chapter in the primary text to reference what the author said about the issue at hand.

"Answers Will Vary"

In the answer section of this study guide you will sometimes come across an answer that reads "answers will vary" for a given question. This generally means that the student is required to answer the question using his/her own knowledge, experience, or intuition. In these instances, the instructor should refer back to the chapter in the primary text to reference what the author said about the issue at hand compared to the student's answer; a "correct" answer should be thoughtful, complete, and on-topic.

Discussion/Essay/Assignment

These assignments are provided so that students can apply the concepts they learned in the given chapter to their own experiences, current events, or historical events — to make the concepts more meaningful. In most cases, it is extremely difficult to "grade" the completed assignments as "right" or "wrong." Instead, the instructor should provide guidance for these assignments. The completeness, thoughtfulness, enthusiasm, and meaning the student brings to the assignment will serve as an indication of the student's mastery of the assignment. If the instructor then wishes to assign a grade, he/she may elect to do so. Or, these assignments may be non-graded "extra credit," serving to boost the student's overall grade for the course.

Uncle Eric's Model of How the World Works

Short Answer/Fill-In/True or False

1. What is a model as defined by Uncle Eric?

2. According to Uncle Eric, why are models important?

3. Why is it important to sort incoming data?

4. Are models rigid? Should they ever change?

5. What are the two models Uncle Eric believes are most reliable, as well as crucially important for everyone to learn? Why does he believe this?

6. _____ is the political philosophy that is no philosophy at all. It embraces the concept that those in power can do whatever appears necessary to achieve their goals.

Discussion/Essay/Assignment

7. Other than Uncle Eric's model, can you provide other examples of models?

8. What purpose does the book ARE YOU LIBERAL? CONSERVATIVE? OR CONFUSED? have relative to Uncle Eric's Model?

9. Listen to, or read, politicians' political speeches, news conferences, news releases, etc., and note if, or how often, the politicians use the phrase "we will do whatever is necessary" to execute a proposal, fix a problem, etc. Do you think it is ever okay to "do whatever is necessary" to resolve a problem? Explain your answer.

10. Look up several of the following words in a dictionary and read their definitions: fascism, liberty, economics, history, republic, and democracy. Does each word have more than one definition? Why?

11. If a word has more than one definition, why is it important that an author define his/her meaning of a word about which he/she is writing?

12. Richard Feynman, a Nobel prize winning physicist, once said it didn't matter what something was called, so long as one understood the characteristics that go into making up what that thing is. It doesn't matter if we call the bird identified as a Blue Jay, "a Blue Jay," so long as we understand that the living creature called by that name has the following characteristics: The bird's food consists primarily of nuts and small seeds as well as insects. They lay from three to six eggs that are blue, green, or yellow with spots of brown or gray. They live for about four years. Another example might be: You might have different names during your lifetime, but you are still the same person. When you are born your parents might name you William. As a child, you might be Billy, or you might

be given a nickname (i.e. Laura Ingalls Wilder from the LITTLE HOUSE™ books was called Half-pint by her Pa). As a teenager you might be Bill or Will, then, as an adult, you might use the more formal William. In all these cases, with all these names, you are still you. If you are female, you might have a maiden name and a married name. Do you agree or disagree with Richard Feynman? Does it matter what something is called, so long as one understands the characteristics of the thing? Explain and provide support for your position.

For Further Reading

13. Read CAPITALISM FOR KIDS by Karl Hess for additional information on different political philosophies, particularly the chapter called "Capitalism and Other Isms." Published by Bluestocking Press, web site: www.BluestockingPress.com; Phone: 800-959-8586.

Author's Disclosure

Short Answer/Fill-In/True or False

1. What is Juris Naturalism?

Discussion/Essay/Assignment

2. In the "Author's Disclosure" Richard Maybury says that few writers disclose the viewpoints or opinions they use to decide what information is important and what is not, or what data will be presented and what data omitted. Collect several history books from your home library, school library, or public library. Do the authors of the books you collected disclose their viewpoints or opinions to the reader? Do the authors disclose what criteria they used to determine what information or data to include in the book and what to omit? Explain why it is, or is not, important to have biases disclosed. What benefit, if any, does a reader or viewer have (in the case of movies, televised news, or documentaries) if he/she is able to determine the viewpoint of a writer?

3. Uncle Eric says all history is slanted based on the facts historians choose to report. Can you provide examples of material you have read or to which you have listened where facts have been reported but perhaps not all the facts? If no books come to mind, have you had arguments or disagreements between siblings or friends in which, when asked, each person presented his/her side of the argument—presenting only those facts that best favored his/her side of the story? How can you learn to identify the slants of writers, news commentators, friends, etc.?

4. Read the quotes in the "Author's Disclosure" section of this book that help to describe the Juris Naturalist viewpoint. Look up the definition of "unalienable" in a current dictionary. Compare a current dictionary's definition with the definition from NOAH WEBSTER'S 1828 DICTIONARY: "Unalienable; that cannot be legally or justly alienated or transferred to another ... All men have certain natural rights which are "inalienable".

5. Samuel Adams defined the natural rights of the colonists as the right to life, liberty, and property. Why do you think "property" was changed to "happiness" in the Declaration of Independence? *(Optional exercise: You can turn this into a research exercise by researching primary source documents of America's Founders to see if you can find the answer for the change from "property" to "happiness." Provide support for your position.)*

6. Select one of the quotes from the "Author's Disclosure" section of this book and write a short essay about what the quote means to you.

For Further Reading

7. Read HOW TO LIE WITH STATISTICS by Darrell Huff, published by W.W. Norton, and distributed by Bluestocking Press, web site: www.BluestockingPress.com; Phone: 800-959-8586. Excellent book. A modern classic. Shows how statistics can distort truth. For ages 14 and up.

8. Read EVALUATING BOOKS: WHAT WOULD THOMAS JEFFERSON THINK ABOUT THIS? an "Uncle Eric" book by Richard J. Maybury. This book provides key indicators and terms to help the reader learn how to identify the slants of authors, media commentators, and others. Published by Bluestocking Press, web site: www.BluestockingPress.com; Phone: 800-959-8586. For ages 12 and up.

9. Secure a copy of WORLD PRESS REVIEW (customer service: PO Box 228, Shrub Oak, New York, 10588, Ph: 914-962-6292). As of this writing, the web site offers a free trial issue for students and educators. The web site is www.worldpressreview.org or email is letters@worldpress.org. Each printed article lists the author and his/her philosophical viewpoint, i.e., Centrist, Libertarian, Liberal, Conservative. Have someone cover up the name and philosophical identity of each author and then read the articles. Can you identify each author's philosophical viewpoint? For help with this exercise, if a student has limited knowledge of political and economic biases, the student should first read Richard J. Maybury's book ARE YOU LIBERAL? CONSERVATIVE? OR CONFUSED? published by Bluestocking Press.

Thought Questions

Before you begin to read ARE YOU LIBERAL? CONSERVATIVE? OR CONFUSED?, answer the following questions. Your answers should be based on your current knowledge and/ or opinions. (If you have no knowledge of the issue/topic, say so.) Save your responses. You will revisit these questions at a later time. After you have answered the questions, you may begin to read ARE YOU LIBERAL? CONSERVATIVE? OR CONFUSED?

1. Explain why you think it is, or is not, a good idea for a writer to disclose his or her philosophical viewpoint or opinions at the beginning of any book, article, or commentary that the writer makes.

2. Has the U.S. Government heeded Washington's advice "to have with [foreign nations] as little political connection as possible"? Explain your answer and provide examples to support your position.

3. Approximately how many political alliances does the U.S. Government have with foreign nations at the time you are reading this question? A good place to begin is with the number of countries in the United Nations, as well as alliances that have been made to fight aggressors of the U.S. Also, research the purpose of the United Nations.

4. How do businesses, churches, charities, and other private institutions get consumers to do what they want?

5. How does government get individuals to do what it wants?

Before Beginning This Book

Ask people to explain to you the basic principles established by America's Founders upon which the USA is founded. Make a list of their answers. Ask how important it is for the original founding principles to be strictly adhered to. If the individuals do not believe the founding principles need to be strictly adhered to, ask what criteria they use to determine when exceptions or changes should be made. Sometimes individuals will remark that the founding principles are too outdated to be relevant to a modern world. Do you agree or disagree with this position?

1. **Controversial Topic Article:** Pretend you are a newspaper reporter. Select a controversial topic. Research all you can about the topic and write a position paper. Save your paper; you will revisit it at a later time.

    IDEAS
    Who was in the right in the Civil War?
    Should the U.S. have involved itself in the Vietnam War?
    Should America have a death penalty?
    Should prayer be permitted in public schools?
    Should there be a separation of school and state?
    Should there be limits on genetic engineering?

2. George Washington said, "Government is not reason; it is not eloquence, it is force. Like fire, it is a dangerous servant and a fearful master." Do you see government as a necessary good or a necessary evil? Explain your answer.

Chapter 1: Don't Be Embarrassed

Thought Questions

Before you begin to read this chapter, complete the following three Thought Questions. Save your answers; you will revisit them later.

1. How would you describe your political and/or party orientation? (i.e. Liberal, Conservative, Centrist, Libertarian, Green, Independent, Democrat, Republican, etc.) If you have no party orientation, explain why.

2. If you identified a political orientation in the preceding question, describe what this label means to you. What is the economic policy consistent with this political philosophy? What model does it follow?

3. Explain what you know about the two predominant political parties in America: Democrat and Republican.

Now begin to read Chapter One. Once you have finished reading the chapter, come back to the study guide and continue to answer the Chapter One questions that follow.

Define

Match the term on the left with its definition on the right. Place the letter of the definition in front of the term to which it corresponds.

_____ 4. Liberal

_____ 5. Conservative

_____ 6. Left

_____ 7. Right

_____ 8. Democrat

_____ 9. Republican

_____ 10. Moderate

_____ 11. Socialist

_____ 12. Communist

_____ 13. Fascist

_____ 14. Libertarian

_____ 15. Centrist

_____ 16. Populist

_____ 17. Common law

_____ 18. Hard science

_____ 19. Editorial

A. Moderate.

B. The system for discovering and applying the Natural Laws that determine the results of human behavior. The system for discovering and applying the Natural Laws that govern the human ecology. The body of definitions and precedents growing from the two fundamental laws that make civilization possible: 1) do all you have agreed to do, and (2) do not encroach on other persons or their property.

C. Originally, a socialist who is striving for the utopia of communism in which there is no government and all live according to the rule, "from each according to his ability, to each according to his needs." Now, one who believes in a dictatorial government that owns and controls everything and everyone.

D. A person on the right side of the left-right political spectrum. Believes in economic freedom and social control.

E. A person on the left side of the political spectrum.

F. A statement of opinion.

G. One who believes there is no real truth and that concepts such as justice and right and wrong are entirely matters of opinion. Also considered nationalists who believe in strong central government that controls everyone according to the rule, "do whatever appears necessary." Often intolerant of minorities.

H. A science in which facts are mathematically measurable and provable through experimentation and observation. Examples: Physics, chemistry, biology, astronomy.

I. The liberal side of the political spectrum.

J. A person on the left side of the left-right political spectrum. Believes in social freedom and economic control.

K. Classical liberal.

L. One who is in the middle of the left-right political spectrum. Advocates both economic encroachment and social encroachment, but perhaps not to the extremes that left and right do.

M. One who is not a democrat or republican but claims to be popular with rank and file voters.

N. A person on the right side of the political spectrum.

O. The conservative side of the political spectrum.

P. A person who advocates socialism. Most have good intentions, they assume government agencies will act in the best interests of the governed, not in the best interests of the government. A Marxist.

Short Answer/Fill-In/True or False

20. Why do American courts use defense attorneys as well as prosecuting attorneys?

21. Why is true objectivity unlikely for a writer?

22. Uncle Eric says the mainstream press resorts to using the left and right political spectrum to report objectively. Uncle Eric says this is wrong on three points. What are these three points?

23. How does Uncle Eric try to avoid the objectivity trap?

24. At the end of Chapter One "Don't Be Embarrassed," how does Uncle Eric refer to his viewpoint?

Discussion/Essay/Assignment

25. Pretend you are a writer for your local newspaper. The "controversial topic" article that you previously wrote before beginning to read this book must be shortened by 50% due to space constraints in the newspaper. For example, if it is a 300-word paper, you must reduce the word count by 50% — to 150 words. Decide how to edit your article by 50% and do so.

26. Now that you've reduced the word count on your "controversial topic" article, make a list of the information that you deleted from the article due to space limitations. Make another list of the information you decided to retain. Save this list.

Chapter 2: The Original American Philosophy

Define

Match the term on the left with its definition on the right. Place the letter of the definition in front of the term to which it corresponds.

_____ 1.   Classical Liberal

_____ 2.   Civil Libertarian

_____ 3.   Juris Naturalis

_____ 4.   Natural Law

_____ 5.   Higher Law

_____ 6.   Law

_____ 7.   Contract law

_____ 8.   Encroach

_____ 9.   Tort law

_____ 10.   Criminal law

_____ 11.   Juris Naturalist

_____ 12.   Juris Naturalism

_____ 13.   Political power

_____ 14.   Government

_____ 15.   State

A. One who believes strongly in the need to protect the individual's rights to free speech, press, religion, assembly, and privacy, but usually not property.

B. Juris Naturalist. One who believes that the country should have a small, weak government, and free markets, and that the individual is endowed by his Creator with inalienable rights to his life, liberty, and property. Also, one who believes in Natural Law and common law, or Higher Law.

C. Law of agreements.

D. Laws enacted by governments. Usually taken to mean laws against violence, fraud, and theft, but, in actual fact, governments tend to criminalize anything they don't like.

E. To intrude on, or damage, the life, liberty, or property of someone who has not harmed anyone. To trespass.

F. An organization with the legal privilege of encroaching on persons who have not harmed anyone.

G. A law higher than any human law.

H. Natural Law.

I. The belief that there is a natural law that determines the results of human conduct and this law is higher than any government's law.

J. Classical liberal. Believes in Higher Law or Natural Law, and that right and wrong are not matters of opinion. Believes political power corrupts both morals and judgment. Wants a government that is small and growing smaller.

K. Broadly speaking, the rules for human conduct which are enforced by violence or threats of violence. More narrowly, sometimes means common law or Natural Law, as distinct from legislation. "A nation of laws and not of men" means a nation in which the highest law is common law or Natural Law, not legislation.

L. The rules that govern the operation of the universe and everything and everyone in it.

M. The legal privilege of encroaching on the life, liberty, or property of a person who has not harmed anyone.

N. Government. Also sometimes means the combination of the government and the country as a single entity.

O. The branch of common law dealing with harm one person does to another.

Short Answer/Fill-In/True or False

16.   What is the name of the political viewpoint that represents the philosophy of America's Founders?

17.   What advice does Uncle Eric give regarding vocabulary and clear communication?

18.   Is Higher Law above, below, or consistent with government's law?

19.   True or False: Higher Law is the belief that right and wrong are not matters of opinion.

20.   True or False: Higher Law can be made up by human beings.

21.   What happens to society, if anything, when governments violate Higher Law?

22.   What are the two laws that are common to all major religions and philosophies?

23.   The origin of the American system of liberty was _____ law.

24.   According to America's Founders, should government be subject to the same principles of Higher Law as individual citizens?

25.   What is a fundamental principle of Higher Law?

26.   Are government and law the same thing?

27.   Does the Juris Naturalist believe government can cease to exist?

28.   What is the most important question for public debate that a Juris Naturalist believes should be asked?

29.   According to the Juris Naturalist, when should government be used to solve problems?

Discussion/Essay/Assignment

30.   Uncle Eric says, "When obedience to Higher Law is widespread, life gets better. When not, life gets worse." Explain why you agree or disagree with this statement.

31.   Can you name any non-government institution that has the legal privilege of using force on persons who have not harmed anyone? (According to the Juris Naturalist, when should government be used to solve problems?)

32.   Describe examples of government encroachment.

33.   Under the Uncle Eric plan, we'd have a constitutional amendment saying lawmakers could not make any new law unless, at the same time, they repealed five. Explain why you think this is a workable solution or not. If you have a better plan, how would your plan work?

For Further Reading

34. DISCOVERY OF FREEDOM by Rose Wilder Lane, published by Fox and Wilkes, San Francisco, CA. Lane examines history relative to individual liberty and human progress. For ages 14 and up.

35. MAINSPRING OF HUMAN PROGRESS by Henry Grady Weaver, published by The Foundation for Economic Education. New York. Condensed version of DISCOVERY OF FREEDOM of listed above. Easier read for ages 12 and up.

36. JONATHAN MAYHEW'S SERMON, published by Bluestocking Press, phone: 800-959-8586, www.BluestockingPress.com. Mayhew challenges individuals to choose between Higher Law and political law.

Chapter 3: The Opposite of the Original American Philosophy

Define

1.   Statist:

Short Answer/Fill-In/True or False

2.   True or False: A statist believes government can perform services in which benefits are greater than total costs.

Discussion/Essay/Assignment

3.   For the next month, create a list of issues that are being discussed by friends, family, the media (newspapers, radio, television), religious leaders, textbook issues, etc. List the issue and the source of comment. Then note whether the source looks to the private sector or to government for a solution to the issue under discussion.

4.   Uncle Eric suggests the following research project: Select any government program you believe is unquestionably good and try to uncover all the hidden costs. Next, match the hidden and unhidden costs against all the benefits. Then determine if you still believe the benefits are greater than the costs.

5.   What is a government subsidy? What bills are paid by your household that have subsidies built into them?

Chapter 4: Basic Political Spectrum

Short Answer/Fill-In/True or False

1. In Congress today, on what side of the room do Democrats sit? Republicans?

2. According to Uncle Eric, what do Liberals emphasize?

3. According to Uncle Eric, what do Conservatives emphasize?

4. Draw a line from the term in the left-hand column to the term in the right-hand column that best describes the position taken during the Vietnam War.

    Liberal   Hawk

    Conservative   Dove

Discussion/Essay/Assignment

5. Explain why you agree or disagree with Uncle Eric that the central issue of the left and right is political power.

Chapter 5: The Nature of Political Power

Define

1. Influence:

Short Answer/Fill-In/True or False

2. Can you think of any institutions, other than government, that can legally use brute force on its "customers" (citizens) to make them buy what it is selling?

3. How did America's Founders try to protect individual citizens from government's political power?

4. What is the difference between political power and influence?

5. If you do not comply with certain political laws you can be taken away by brute force or your property can be confiscated. List at least five examples of these political laws.

For Research

6. If you are studying about political philosophies during an election campaign, make a list of Conservative candidates' issues and a list of Liberal candidates' issues. Uncle Eric says

liberals generally support laws against guns and laws supporting social security. Conservatives, he says, generally support military conscription and laws against drug use. Does your list support or refute Uncle Eric's conclusions? If there is no current election campaign, then research candidates' issues from a prior presidential election of your choice.

7.   See if you can locate any statements made by America's Founders in support of democracy. Be sure to note your source/s. (i.e. author, title of source, date of publication, page number on which reference is found.) Do the same for references in support of liberty. Can you find negative comments by America's Founders about democracy or majority rule?

To View

8.   HARRY'S WAR starring Edward Hermann, Geraldine Page, Karen Grassle, David Odgen Stiers. Harry Johnson, a mild-mannered postman, declares war on the Internal Revenue Service because they unfairly bill his "Aunt" Beverly over $192,000 in back taxes. Emphasis is on the lack of rights taxpayers have when confronted by the excessive abuse of power that is exercised by the IRS. All Harry wants is a trial by his peers as guaranteed by the Constitution. Harry asks, "Is the IRS above the Constitution of the United States?" Harry remarks that if he were accused of murder he'd have more rights than he'd know what to do with, but when audited by the IRS they make you think you have no rights whatsoever. In this movie, Harry has gone to war against the abuse of power that is exercised by the IRS. He says, "They (the IRS) make their own laws, and they administer them, and they enforce them, and they prosecute them, and they judge them. All that power in one place...Boy, Hitler would have loved the IRS. So would Napolean and Caesar...Government doesn't have any right to do anything but what we give it. And they're supposed to protect us from what the IRS is doing — in the name of government." Comedy/drama (1981). 98 min. PG

Chapter 6: The Two Categories of Encroachment

Define

1.   Wealth:

Short Answer/Fill-In/True or False

2.   How would the Juris Naturalist attempt to solve the problems of poverty, drug addiction, education of children, etc.?

Discussion/Essay/Assignment

3.   Uncle Eric states that liberals are Juris Naturalists in social matters, but they tend to be statists in economic matters. Conservatives tend to be Juris Naturalists in economic matters and statists in social matters. He says the best way to determine another person's

political philosophy is to listen for opinions on a wide range of issues. A touchstone for pinpointing whether a person is truly a Juris Naturalist is to discover on what issues the individual is willing to use government force. Make a list of issues (you can include those listed in this chapter), and ask individuals who are willing to participate in your research assignment, what their position is on each issue on your list. There are no right or wrong answers. You are collecting data. Sometimes people have not given deep thought to the consistency of their political beliefs, so the data you collect might indicate an individual is not completely consistent with a particular political ideology.

4.   Make a list of "Campaign Issues" from a current or prior presidential campaign. (Keep this list, you will be asked to revisit it in future questions.) Beside each issue, place the name of the candidates who ran for president (Democrat, Republican, and any other party candidates you wish to include). Indicate if the candidate was for or against the issue. Make another column that represents America's Founders. Indicate whether you believe the Founders would be for or against the issue. Your column headings should be:

Issue   Candidate#1 For/Against   Candidate #2 For/Against   America's Founders For/Against

How does your list compare to the issues list compiled by Uncle Eric in the chapter "Two Categories of Encroachment"?

Money - Liberals encroach   Social - Conservatives encroach

For Research

5.   An ambitious research project is to trace the history of political parties in this country. You will discover through this process how political parties have evolved, how political party names have changed, why some individuals changed their party affiliations even though their ideologies did not change (i.e. The South was strongly in favor of state's rights, which is traditionally a Republican issue. However, the South, as a whole, is today considered Democratic territory. Why? The answer: When Lincoln was elected President, many voters in the South switched to the Democratic Party ticket. List your research sources.)

Chapter 7: The Middle Ground

Short Answer/Fill-In/True or False

1.   What is another name for Moderate?

2.   What does a Moderate position represent?

3.   Regarding economic and social conduct, what is the Moderate position?

4.   How do Moderates behave regarding privacy?

5.   True or False: The total amount of power a Moderate wishes to hold over another person is equal to or less than that desired by either left or right.

Chapter 8: Freedom vs. Liberty

Define

1.   Freedom:

2.   Liberty:

Short Answer/Fill-In/True or False

3.   According to Thomas Jefferson, liberty is a right endowed by the Creator and cannot be revoked by anyone but the Creator or oneself. How can an individual revoke his/her own liberty?

Discussion/Essay/Assignment

4.   Name some famous outlaws from the days of the wild west. What did they do to deserve the title of "outlaw"?

5.   For at least one month, as you read textbooks, listen to the media, and read newspapers, keep a list of how often the term "liberty" is used versus how often the term "freedom" is used, as well as in what context the terms are used.

6.   Liberty, according to Thomas Jefferson is "unobstructed action according to our will within limits drawn around us by the equal rights of others." The 1828 WEBSTER'S DICTIONARY defines Natural Liberty: "Natural liberty, consists in the power of acting as one thinks fit, without any restraint or control, except from the laws of nature. It is a state of exemption from the control of others, and from positive laws and the institutions of social life. This liberty is abridged by the establishment of government." Look up the definition of 'liberty" and/or "natural liberty" in a modern dictionary. Compare the modern definition to Webster's definition. Explain the differences, if any.

7.   In a democracy the argument can be made that citizens make choices based on their exercise of free vote and that they agree to be bound legally by the outcome of a vote, whether or not they agree with the outcome. Why were America's Founders afraid of democracy and the crowd mentality?

8.   In FEDERALIST PAPER # 10 James Madison wrote, "Such democracies have ever been spectacles of turbulence and contention; have ever been found incompatible with personal security or the rights of property, and have in general been as short in their lives as they have been violent in their deaths." America was founded as a republic, not a democracy.

For the next month, keep track of the number of times America is referred to as a democracy versus the number of times it is referred to as a republic. Why is this distinction important?

For Further Study

9. For further study on the topic of inalienable rights listen TO COMMON SENSE AND THE DECLARATION OF INDEPENDENCE, an audio history product produced by Knowledge Products, Nashville, TN, and distributed by Bluestocking Press, web site: www.BluestockingPress.com or phone: 800-959-8586.

Chapter 9: Exceptions

Define

1. Socialism:

Short Answer/Fill-In/True or False

2. According to Uncle Eric, how is liberty usually lost?

Discussion/Essay/Assignment

3. With what political philosophy do you identify? Do you agree 100% with that party's philosophy/platform, and if not, where do you disagree?

4. Thomas Jefferson was afraid that government would make exceptions to the principles that make liberty possible. Thomas Jefferson said, "A departure from principle in one instance becomes a precedent for a second; that second for a third; and so on, till the bulk of society is reduced to mere automatons of misery, to have no sensibilities left but for sinning and suffering." Jefferson also said, "Only lay down true principles and adhere to them inflexibly." No exceptions — exceptions lead to a destruction of liberty. Do you agree or disagree? Support your position.

5. Liberty, according to Uncle Eric, is best achieved by adhering to the two fundamental laws: 1) do all you have agreed to do, and 2) do not encroach on other persons of their property. Review the list of campaign issues that you compiled. Next, make two columns, one for each of the fundamental laws. If any of the campaign issues would violate either of these fundamental laws, list the issue under the law that it would violate.

6. Are any of the "Campaign issues" that you compiled (chapter 6, question #4) inconsistent with the strict definition of Liberal or Conservative as defined by Uncle Eric? Make two columns: one Liberal, the other Conservative. List the issues that appear inconsistent with the political party's philosophy.

   Liberal   Conservative

Do your findings explain where the current terms of a moderate Liberal or moderate Conservative come from? What other terms have you heard that define an inconsistency with the pure definition of Liberal and Conservative?

7. Compare the U.S. today to the U.S. in 1800. How many liberties have we lost? A good place to start is with taxes. How many taxes do we have compared to 1800? Can you recall any tax that has been levied that was not levied with the best of intentions?

Chapter 10: Military and Foreign Policy

Short Answer/Fill-In/True or False

1. Prior to the collapse of the former Soviet Empire, what was the liberal position on foreign policy and military aid? What was the one exception liberals allowed regarding foreign policy?

2. Prior to the collapse of the former Soviet Empire, what did Conservatives allow regarding foreign policy?

3. What is the Juris Naturalist position about foreign intervention?

4. Name some wars from the 20th century in which the U.S. participated.

5. What does Uncle Eric mean when he says that the Bill of Rights stops at the U.S. borders?

6. What is the difference between an isolationist versus an individual who believes in political neutrality?

7. Was George Washington an isolationist?

Discussion/Essay/Assignment

8. Uncle Eric states that since the collapse of the Soviet Empire, neither Liberals nor Conservatives have a clear idea of their foreign policies. Keep a list of foreign policy issues that are discussed in the media. Then make a list of whether all Liberals or Conservatives are for or against the issue; or whether some Liberals and some Conservatives are for the issue and others against — creating a split within their own political party.

9. Explain why you agree or disagree with the Juris Naturalist position that if you travel or do business abroad you should do so at your own risk and should not expect the U.S. military to rescue you from a situation you entered voluntarily (the lives of American troops should not be risked).

10. Explain why you agree or disagree with George Washington's warning to Americans in his FAREWELL ADDRESS, that: "The great rule of conduct for us, in regard to foreign nations, is, in extending our commercial relations, to have with them as little political connections as possible. So far as we have already formed engagements, let them be fulfilled with perfect good faith. Here let us stop."

11. How many known alliances has George W. Bush made in his efforts to fight terrorists? What do you think George Washington would say about this?

12. Travel warnings are issued when the U.S. State Department recommends that Americans avoid a certain country. Visit the U.S. Department of State "travel warning" web site, which, at the time I write this in 2004, is located at http://travel.state.gov/warnings_list.html. At the time I write this, 27 countries are included in the Travel Warning list. An additional 12 countries are listed that "pose significant risks or disruptions to Americans," in addition, a worldwide caution is posted on this list. How many countries are listed at the time you check the Travel Warnings web site, and where are they located on a world map?

Chapter 11: Democrats and Republicans

Define

1. Democrat:

2. Republican:

3. Capitalist:

4. Capitalism:

Short Answer/Fill-In/True or False

5. In the U.S. what is the party of the left?

6. In the U.S. what is the party of the right?

7. Where do the Democrats and Republicans usually hover on the political spectrum and why?

8. Do you think where the Democrats and Republicans hover on the political spectrum might explain why it's difficult to differentiate candidates representing the two parties during an election?

9. What is another word for free markets?

10.   What are the two types of capitalists described by Uncle Eric?

11.   What is the result of the capitalist who says he/she believes in capitalism but doesn't follow the philosophy?

Discussion/Essay/Assignment

12.   Conduct a survey of friends and family. Ask what economic group in the U.S. they believe Democrats and Republicans tend to represent? Are their answers consistent with Uncle Eric's conclusion that most people consider the Democrats to be the party of the poor and the Republicans the party of the rich?

13.   Uncle Eric agrees with America's Founders that government, by its very nature, will continue to grow and increase its political power. Every political party attempts to gain greater control, hence more power, which means that the sum total of government will always grow and gain more power. Do you agree or disagree, and why?

14.   Read the following quotes from America's Founders. Explain where they agree or disagree with Uncle Eric.

"It will not be denied that power is of an encroaching nature."
                    — James Madison, Federalist Paper #48

"I am more and more convinced that man is a dangerous creature and that power, whether vested in many or a few, is ever grasping, and, like the grave, cries 'Give, give.'" — Abigail Adams

"I know no safe depository of the ultimate powers of the society but the people themselves; and if we think them not enlightened enough to exercise their control with a wholesome discretion, the remedy is not to take it from them but to inform their discretion." — Thomas Jefferson

"Government is not reason; it is not eloquence; it is force. Like fire, it is a dangerous servant and a fearful master."   — George Washington

"...a wise and frugal government, which shall restrain men from injuring one another, which shall leave them otherwise free to regulate their own pursuits of industry and improvement, and shall not take from the mouth of labor the bread it has earned. This is the sum of good government."
                    — Thomas Jefferson, first inaugural address 1801

For Further Reading

15.   CAPITALISM FOR KIDS by Karl Hess. Highly recommended. Explains the strict definition of capitalism, introduces young people to the benefits of entrepreneurship, and provides a quiz to help the reader determine if he/she has the temperament to be an entrepreneur.

Also explains the other isms: communism, socialism, fascism, etc. Ages 9 and up. Published by Bluestocking Press, web site: www.BluestockingPress.com, phone: 800-959-8586

16. THE PRESIDENT'S CABINET AND HOW IT GREW by Nancy Winslow Parker. Ages 8-10. Published by Harper, a children's book about the first Cabinet and its growth since the beginning. What positions, if any, have been added to the President's Cabinet since this book was written? (The latter question will require research.)

Chapter 12: Socialism and Communism

Define

1. Liberalism:

2. Socialist:

3. Marxism:

4. Marxist:

5. Welfare statism:

Short Answer/Fill-In/True or False

6. What is the popular meaning and economic objective of a Socialist?

7. What is the popular meaning of a communist and what countries are examples of the communist economic system?

8. True or False: The early American colonies were founded on the system of mercantilism.

9. What form of socialism is most commonly found in the United States today?

10. Name some examples of welfare statism programs in the U.S. today.

11. In what decade did the U.S. begin to implement socialist programs?

12. What event caused U.S. citizens to change from their traditionally "we must take care of ourselves" philosophy to "we must look to government to take care of us."

Discussion/Essay/Assignment

13. Identify and explain the six stages of Karl Marx's dialectical materialism.

14. Uncle Eric says that the system in the former Soviet Union was called communism and was seen as cruel and warlike, while many saw socialism as gentle and caring, a way to fight poverty. The former Soviet Union was socialist, not communist, which created confusion regarding the philosophical definition and distinction between communism and socialism. While fighting "communism," Conservatives often permitted socialist programs in the U.S. to be passed. What is one example of such a program?

15. Uncle Eric says that Conservatives were so busy fighting what they believed was communism that they did little to stop the shift toward socialism. If you know people who lived through the events of the Great Depression, ask as many of them as you can what they remember about the implementation of the Social Security program. Is their recollection different in any way from Uncle Eric's explanation?

To View

16. GUILTY BY SUSPICION, starring Robert De Niro, Annette Bening. Recreates Hollywood's famous "Blacklist Era." A period when careers were ruined by friends and colleagues who named suspected Communists. Shows the fear of Communism that raged in the U.S. following World War II. Rated PG-13.

Chapter 13: Fascism

Define

1. Fascism:

2. Fascist:

Short Answer/Fill-In/True or False

3. What causes fascism to be unique among the "isms"?

4. Draw a line from the intellectual leader in the left column to the "ism" in the right column to which each leader is most closely identified.

John Maynard Keynes	welfare statists
Karl Marx	Conservatives
America's Founders	Juris Naturalists
Adam Smith	Socialists
No intellectual leader	Fascists

5.   What is the basic premise of fascism?

6.   Name individuals who were fascist leaders.

7.   Define pragmatism as it relates to fascists.

8.   What does Uncle Eric mean when he says fascists are masters of disguise?

9.   What is the key element needed to keep a powerholder in check?

Discussion/Essay/Assignment

10.   Do you believe the internment of Japanese-Americans who were American citizens in World War II was a violation of the Bill of Rights? Support your position. (For further reading on this topic see For Further Reading section that follows.)

11.   The system of checks and balances put into place in the U.S. by America's Founders was an attempt to restrain the growth of government and the abuses of government. The judicial branch was the "right and wrong" branch of government. If a policyholder allowed a law to pass that was not ethically correct the judicial arm of government was to correct the error. What happens to a system of checks and balances if the judicial arm of government stops using Higher Law as the touchstone for truth? (For further reading on the subject of Higher Law see WHATEVER HAPPENED TO JUSTICE? and THE LAW — see For Further Reading in the section that follows.)

12.   In 1816 Thomas Jefferson said, "A departure from principle in one instance becomes a precedent for a second, that second for a third; and so on, till the bulk of society is reduced to mere automatons of misery, to have no sensibilities left but for sinning and suffering." Explain why you agree or disagree with Jefferson.

For Research

13.   Uncle Eric says that the principle for which Hitler was fighting, fascism, survived even though Hitler died, and now fascism is sweeping the world. Do you agree or disagree? Spend the next 30 days recording statements from U.S. political/government officials and political candidates. Listen for the phrase "we will do whatever is necessary to achieve our objectives." Make three columns. In the first column list the individual's name who makes the statement. In the second column list his/her political affiliation. In the third column list the issue to which the politician refers. If you have access to several television or radio stations, try to listen to liberal as well as conservative programming. What conclusions can you draw at the end of this 30-day research project? (This project will be easier to research during an election period or during a crisis period in the U.S.A.: flood, hurricane, threat of war, war).

For Further Reading (about the Japanese Internment)

14.   BASEBALL SAVED US by Ken Mochizuki. Surrounded by guards, fences, and a desert, Japanese-Americans in an internment camp create a baseball field to give themselves a positive activity — providing purpose in an environment of injustice. For ages 5-10. Published by Lee and Low Books, Inc. New York.

15.   FAREWELL TO MANZANAR by Jeanne Wakatsuki Houston & James D. Houston. True story of a Japanese-American family's attempt to survive the indignities of forced detention at Manzanar. For ages 12 and up. Published by Dell Laurel-Leaf, New York.

16.   JOURNEY TO TOPAZ by Yoshiko Uchida. Yuki, 11 years old, is shipped to the desert concentration camp called Topaz. Based on the author's personal experience. For ages 10 and up. Published by Creative Arts Book Company.

17.   Read the personal account of Roy Uyeda and his family, which details the violations of Constitutional rights by the U.S. Government during World War II. Distributed by Bluestocking Press, phone: 800-959-8586; web site: www.BluestockingPress.com

To read more about Higher Law, a suggested reading list follows:

18.   WHATEVER HAPPENED TO JUSTICE? by Richard J. Maybury, an Uncle Eric book, published by Bluestocking Press, phone: 800-959-8586; web site: www.BluestockingPress.com. In very clear language explains America's legal history; how our common law heritage has been replaced by political law and the economic impact of that. Ages 14 up.

19.   THE LAW by Frederic Bastiat. Written in 1850, this small book provides an excellent explanation of the source and purpose of government. Ages 14 up. Distributed by Bluestocking Press, web site: www.BluestockingPress.com, phone: 800-959-8586.

20.   COMMON LAW by Oliver Wendell Holmes. A classic history of the law from Roman times to present times written in layman's language. Ages 16 up. Published by Dover Publications.

Chapter 14: What Are They Really?

For Research/Discussion

1.   In Uncle Eric's Capital Risk Test he suggests that before you invest any money in a country ask seven questions. The first is "Does a nation have a constitution or some other legal safeguard based at least approximately on the fundamental principles of the old British common law?" In his Uncle Eric book, WHATEVER HAPPENED TO PENNY CANDY, Richard Maybury lists countries throughout the world and the type of legal system on which each country is based. It is suggested that you secure a copy of this book and read the list. In doing so, note how many countries are based on Higher Law/old English common law versus how many are not. Also, if the country does not pass Uncle Eric's Capital Risk Test, would you want to travel in that country?

2.   Uncle Eric suggests the following research project: How many Marines have died protecting American liberty? How many have died protecting someone's foreign investments? A good place to start is with the list of 137 United States military actions since 1798 on page 24 of the January 15, 1987 WALL STREET JOURNAL.

For Further Reading

3.   WHATEVER HAPPENED TO PENNY CANDY by Richard J. Maybury, particularly Chapter 15 "Natural Law and Economic Prosperity," published by Bluestocking Press, web site: www.BluestockingPress.com, phone: 800-959-8586.

Chapter 15: The Other Middle View

Short Answer/Fill-In/True or False

1.   In what way do Moderates combine the political positions of the left and right?

2.   In what way do Juris Naturalists combine the political positions of the left and right?

3.   Juris Naturalists are terrified of _____ _____.

4.   How was the Federal government financed prior to the 20th century?

For Research/Discussion

5.   Uncle Eric says that America's Founders believed in Higher Law and liberty, however, they had difficulty adhering to the standard that they themselves set. For research, follow the careers of those American Founders who held political office. In what ways, if any, did they violate their own founding principles? Presidents include: George Washington, John Adams, Thomas Jefferson, James Madison. Which of these were Federalists and which were anti-Federalists? Did their political positions on Federalism make a difference in how strictly they adhered to the original founding principles?

6.   Ask any person who is willing to participate the following questions regarding political philosophy. What conclusions, if any, can you draw, based on their answers?

     a. What is your political orientation?
     b. On what issues, if any, do you disagree with your party?
     c. What are the basic moral principles of your political party?
     d. Where do you draw the line you believe the government should not cross?

Chapter 16: The National Religion

Short Answer/Fill-In/True or False

1.   Uncle Eric says the Juris Naturalist wants the same things everyone else does, including elimination of poverty and unemployment, as well as good education for children. Where does the Juris Naturalist viewpoint differ from other political viewpoints?

2.   What does Uncle Eric believe is the root cause of poverty, business failures, unemployment, etc.?

3.   What does Uncle Eric believe is the only real solution to our country's problems?

Discussion/Essay/Assignment

4.   Before the U.S. Government grew to the size it is today, how did people go about solving their problems: 1) as an individual? 2) as a community? Ask relatives and friends who lived during the first half of the 20th century how problems were solved. Ask what the pros and/or cons are between government solutions versus private solutions based on any first-hand experiences or observations they may have.

5.   Uncle Eric said that early American churches were the center of the communities and the clergy were the community leaders. When problems arose, people met at their local houses of worship to organize solutions. Can you think of any stories you have read or films you have viewed that reflect this observation by Uncle Eric?

6.   Is there any group of individuals today that might still rely on themselves rather than government to solve their problems?

7.   In the 1990s a popular term was "empowerment." Is it still the word of choice today? If, not, what word or phrase has replaced the term "empowerment"?

8.   An expression that grew from actual practice is "You can do business on a handshake." What does this mean? What is the chance that this can happen today? Where is it most likely to occur?

Chapter 17: A U.S.-Nazi Alliance or a U.S.-Soviet Alliance?

Short Answer/Fill-In/True or False

1. Draw a line connecting the political position in the left column that most closely matches the viewpoint on the right, when, in the 1930s, the U.S. political leaders had to decide whose side they should take in the war?

     left   fascism / Hitler

     Juris Naturalist   socialism / Stalin

     right   political neutrality / America's Founders

2. With whom did America's political leaders form an alliance during World War II and with what political policy was that leader identified?

3. According to Uncle Eric, why was the leftist view most popular in America?

4. What is the difference between a person who wants isolationism versus one who wants political neutrality?

Discussion/Essay/Assignment

5. Do you favor a position of isolationism, political neutrality, or political alliances? Explain your reasons for the position you favor.

For Further Reading

6. THE WORLD WAR SERIES: 1) THE THOUSAND YEAR WAR IN THE MIDEAST: HOW IT AFFECTS YOU TODAY; 2) WORLD WAR I: THE REST OF THE STORY AND HOW IT AFFECTS YOU TODAY and, 3) WORLD WAR II: THE REST OF THE STORY AND HOW IT AFFECTS YOU TODAY, all by Richard J. Maybury, an Uncle Eric book, published by Bluestocking, web site: www.BluestockingPress.com, phone: 800-959-8586. Excellent explanations of alliances, political neutrality, and Franklin Roosevelt's move towards socialism in the 1930s and 1940s.

7. WASHINGTON'S FAREWELL ADDRESS (1796) by George Washington. Washington encourages political neutrality. At the time of this writing, a copy was posted at the following Internet site: www.yale.edu/lawweb/avalon/washing.htm
    If it is no longer there, do a web search for another listing source.

Chapter 18: Economic Counterparts

Define

1.   Keynesianism:

2.   Monetarism:

3.   Austrian economics:

4.   Laissez faire capitalism:

Short Answer/Fill-In/True or False

5.   In what year was income tax created?

6.   Prior to income tax, from where did the Federal government receive most of its tax revenue?

7.   In 1995, what percentage of the government's receipts came from liquor, tobacco, and imports? Where does the balance of the Federal government's receipts come from?

8.   True or False: Government spends much of its time redistributing the money it collects which causes economic philosophy to be a huge part of political philosophy.

9.   What is the economics of the far left called?

10.   What is the economics of the center-left (Democrats, Welfare Statists, and Moderates) called?

11.   What is the economics of the right called?

12.   What is the economics of the extreme right called?

13.   What is the economics of the Juris Naturalist called?

14.   What was the dominant economic policy during America's first 150 years?

Discussion/Essay/Assignment

15.   Uncle Eric suggests you try to answer the following: Should there be an upper limit to taxation? If so, how much of a family's income do you think the government should be able to take before it is excessive or becomes theft?

For Further Reading

16.   CAPITALISM FOR KIDS by Karl Hess. An excellent explanation of laissez faire capitalism compared to other economic philosophies, written for ages 10 and up. Published by Bluestocking Press, web site: www.BluestockingPress.com, phone: 800-959-8586.

Chapter 19: Effects on Your Money

Define

1.   Communist:

Short Answer/Fill-In/True or False

2.   According to Uncle Eric, how do leftist/Liberal political philosophies affect your money?

3.   What perception do Liberals have regarding private business?

4.   What are the potential repercussions to employees whose employers have been taxed by liberal programs?

5.   What effect can leftist monetary policy have on investment markets?

6.   Uncle Eric says Conservatives have a better understanding of economics so are less likely to interfere in your work, business, or investments. However, name the two other areas where they are likely to interfere.

7.   What are Uncle Eric's conclusions about the dangers of conservatism and liberalism?

8.   What does Uncle Eric say the Juris Naturalist wants?

Discussion/Essay/Assignment

9.   Sometimes individuals will close their business or quit their work because government programs make it too expensive or too difficult to want to continue. Do you know anyone who has quit one type of work because of government controls on his/her field of work or because of the cost of doing business due to government programs and taxation? Ask your parents, relatives, and friends if they know any persons like this. What type of work was being done, and what is that person doing today? Do you know anyone who chose to retire early rather than continue to work because he/she did not want to continue to pay what they perceived to be excessive taxes? Do you know anyone who is avoiding going into a field of work because of the government controls associated with that type of work?

10. If you know any people who are self-employed, ask them how many hours per year they spend on government paperwork. Ask what they would do with the additional time and money if government paperwork and taxes were eliminated (or drastically reduced).

11. Do you know anyone who has lost his/her job because an employer switched to machinery or sent the work overseas? Often in these cases the employer, or American business as a category, is blamed for not providing jobs in America. What might be wrong in a country where business finds it less expensive to send work out of its own country even while incurring the costs to import the product back into the country; where business finds it cheaper to produce a product outside America rather than producing that same product on homeland soil or with the labor of its own citizens? Select a business that manufactures overseas and try to determine/research why the business chose to manufacture overseas rather than on homeland soil.

12. Following the attacks on the World Trade Center and the Pentagon on September 11, 2001, the U.S. Government began enacting new policies (i.e. The Patriot Act) in an effort to protect Americans from further terrorist attacks. Controversy has followed because with the enactment of new policies, personal privacy has been reduced. What do you think are the short and long-term ramifications of the post 9-11 government policies?

13. Uncle Eric observes that most news stories and political and economic analyses today are based on the left-right political spectrum — Liberals versus Conservatives. Uncle Eric advises that, instead, you focus on political power versus liberty. Where is power winning or losing and where is liberty winning or losing? Keep a record of news stories over the next one or two months. Note the issue, and also note if the solution will result in more government control or greater personal liberty. Finally, note if the source of the issue (control vs. liberty) is from the left or right of the political spectrum.

Chapter 20: Three Types of Wrongdoing

Define

1. Manners:

2. Tort:

Short Answer/Fill-In/True or False

3. Of the three types of wrongdoing identified by Uncle Eric, name the type that warrants intervention by law and explain what it is.

4. What is the most important idea separating Juris Naturalists from others?

Chapter 21: Muddied Waters

Define

1. Anarchism:

2. Terrorism:

3. Politicize:

4. Warlord:

5. Populist:

6. Bolshevik:

7. Nationalist:

8. Civil Libertarian:

9. Radical, Extremist, Fanatic:

Short Answer/Fill-In

10. What is Uncle Eric's advice regarding word usage?

Discussion/Essay/Assignment

11. From this point forward, try to implement the advice given by Uncle Eric: In a discussion, always try to explain the terms you are using so that the person/s with whom you have entered a discussion clearly understand your definition of the word/s you are using. In like manner, if someone with whom you are conversing fails to define his/her terms, ask that individual for a clear definition of terms. See if this effort on your part diminishes the number of misunderstandings and makes for clearer communication.

Chapter 22: Who Gets the Children?

Discussion/Essay/Assignment

1. This chapter is about bigotry. What terms can you list that have been used to identify ethnic groups in American over the past century? Do ethnic labels contribute to bigotry in a society? Explain.

Chapter 23: The Return of Racism

Discussion/Essay/Assignment

1. For the next month make notes regarding any remarks, comments, laws, legislation, writings, commentaries, music lyrics, legislation, and/or policy decisions that refer to race, creed, or color. Include what would be considered pro and con remarks. What conclusions can you draw from your observations?

2. For the next month, make notes of how often an individual is celebrated and identified as an individual, rather than identified with a group, race, religion, culture, etc. What conclusions can you draw from your observations?

Chapter 24: The First American Philosophies

Short Answer/Fill-In/True or False

1. What observation does Uncle Eric make about Patrick Henry and James Madison?

2. Explain the fears that James Madison and Patrick Henry had regarding government.

3. On the subject of government, where did James Madison and Patrick Henry agree?

Discussion/Essay/Assignment

4. Write an essay explaining the differences between the Federalist and anti-Federalist political philosophy.

5. Uncle Eric says that he suspects that the conflict between the Federalists and anti-Federalists led to both sides inventing a better system of government than either alone would have. Explain why you agree or disagree with Uncle Eric's conclusion.

6. The Federalists advocated a strong federal government. The anti-Federalists believed in states' rights and were responsible for the Bill of Rights — the first ten amendments to the Constitution. Locate a few public school history textbooks. Compare how these public school textbooks explain the differences between the Federalists and anti-Federalists. What conclusions, if any, can you make?

7. Article X of the Bill of Rights says, "The powers not delegated to the United States by the Constitution, nor prohibited by it to the States, are reserved to the States respectively, or to the people." Why do you think this amendment is significant?

For Further Reading

8.   THE CONSTITUTION OF THE UNITED STATES.

9.   THE FEDERALIST PAPERS. Edited by Clinton Rossiter. Defends the concept of a strong central government. Published by Penguin Putnam. Ages 14 and up.

10. THE ANTI-FEDERALIST PAPERS. Edited by Ralph Ketcham. The anti-Federalists believed in states rights. Published by Penguin Putnam. Ages 14 and up.

Chapter 25: Summary

Short Answer/Fill-In/True or False

1.   On what should you focus your attention in order to understand political philosophies?

2.   What political philosophical groups are active seekers of political power?

3.   What political philosophy wants to minimize political power and increase individual liberty?

4.   What term, according to Uncle Eric, best describes Liberals, Moderates, and Conservatives?

5.   What do Liberals want to control?

6.   What do Conservatives want to control?

7.   What do Moderates want to control?

8.   What do Juris Naturalists want to control?

9.   What are the two fundamental laws that make civilization possible?

10. What political philosophy did America's Founders embrace?

11. Uncle Eric states that whenever you read anything, except math or the "hard" sciences, you are reading an editorial. What causes him to draw this conclusion?

Discussion/Essay/Assignment/Research

12. If possible, get a copy (check with your library or the publisher) of WORLD PRESS REVIEW magazine, PO Box 228, Shrub Oak, NY 10588-9918, web site: www.worldpress.org. WORLD PRESS REVIEW reprints articles from different sources and generally discloses the viewpoints of the authors of the articles. Try to identify the slants of writers of your daily newspaper, or news commentators, or literature, etc.

13. Are school history books objective? Locate some history textbooks and select a few topics to maintain consistency for your comparison from textbook to textbook. For example, how does the author explain: Franklin Roosevelt and the New Deal; the reason/s for the Civil War; how well reported is the position of the Loyalists versus the Patriots during the American Revolution; what is championed more by the author: individuality or unity? Are America's founding principles thoroughly explained: limited government, international neutrality, free market economics, and Higher Law principles? Is the emphasis on America as a democracy or is the emphasis on America as a republic? Is any mention made about America's legal heritage: old English common law?

14. For research, try to locate old textbooks, prior to 1940. Also, be aware of old movies, prior to WWII, as well as literature. Compare how the writers view government before the 1940s as well as after. What conclusions can you draw? Try to identify the writer's slant.

Chapter 26: Encroachment: Big and Small

Discussion/Essay/Assignment

1. The first fundamental law is: Do not encroach on other persons or their property. For two weeks keep track of the number of encroachments you identify, large and small, that affect your life.

Final Exam Questions

(Numbers 1 – 50 are worth 2 points each)

1. Define: Liberal

2. Define: Conservative

3. True or False: A Democrat is a person on the left side of the political spectrum.

4. True or False: A Republican is a person on the right side of the political spectrum.

5. Define: Socialist

6. Define: Common law

7. Uncle Eric says the mainstream press resorts to using the left and right political spectrum to report objectively. Uncle Eric says this is wrong on three points. What are these three points?

8. Define: Classical Liberal

9. Define: Juris Naturalism

10. Define: Political power

11. Is Higher Law above, below, or consistent with government's law?

12. True or False: Higher Law can be made up by human beings.

13. According to Uncle Eric, what are the two laws that are common to all major religions and philosophies?

14. What is the most important question for public debate that a Juris Naturalist believes should be asked?

15. According to the Juris Naturalist, when should government be used to solve problems?

16. True or False: A statist believes government can perform services in which benefits are greater than total costs.

17. What is the difference between political power and influence?

18. How would the Juris Naturalist attempt to solve the problems of poverty, drug addiction, education of children, etc.?

19. True or False: The total amount of power a Moderate wishes to hold over another person is equal to or less than that desired by either left or right.

20. According to Thomas Jefferson, liberty is a right endowed by the Creator and cannot be revoked by anyone but the Creator or oneself. How can an individual revoke his/her own liberty?

21. Define: Freedom

22. Define: Liberty

23. According to Uncle Eric, how is liberty usually lost?

24. What is the Juris Naturalist position about foreign intervention?

25. What is the difference between an isolationist and an individual who believes in political neutrality?

26. What are the two types of capitalists described by Uncle Eric?

27. What is the result of the capitalist who says he believes in capitalism but doesn't follow the philosophy?

28. What is the popular meaning and economic objective of a Socialist?

29. What form of socialism is the most common found in the United States today?

30. In what decade did the U.S. begin to implement socialist programs?

31. What event caused U.S. citizens to change from their traditionally "we must take care of ourselves" philosophy to "we must look to government to take care of us"?

32. Identify the six stages of Karl Marx's dialectical materialism.

33. Define: Fascist

34. What does Uncle Eric mean when he says fascists are masters of disguise?

35. What is the key element needed to keep a powerholder in check?

36. In what way do Moderates combine the political positions of the left and right?

37. In what way do Juris Naturalists combine the political positions of the left and right?

38. Uncle Eric says the Juris Naturalist wants the same things everyone else does, including elimination of poverty, unemployment, as well as good education for children. Where does the Juris Naturalist viewpoint differ from other political viewpoints?

39. With whom did America's political leaders form an alliance during World War II and with what political policy was that leader identified?

40. According to Uncle Eric, why was the leftist view most popular in America?

41. What is the difference between a person who wants isolationism versus a person who wants political neutrality?

42. What is the economics of the far left called?

43. What is the economics of center-left (Democrats, Welfare Statists, and Moderates) called?

44. What was the dominant economic policy during America's first 150 years?

45. Uncle Eric says Conservatives have a better understanding of economics so are less likely to interfere in your work, business, or investments. However, name the two other areas where they are likely to interfere.

46. What is the most important idea separating Juris Naturalists from others?

47. On the subject of government, where did James Madison and Patrick Henry agree?

48. What term, according to Uncle Eric, best describes Liberals, Moderates, and Conservatives?

49. Uncle Eric states that whenever you read anything, except math or the "hard" sciences, you are reading an editorial. What causes him to draw this conclusion?

50. Explain what the most important idea is that you have learned from reading this book?

Final Exercises (#51 and #52 worth 25 points each)

51. Before you began to read this book you wrote a "Controversial Topic Article." Now that you have finished this book, reread your "Controversial Topic Article." Would you make any changes in your paper? Explain what changes you would make and why. If you would make no changes, explain why you are satisfied with your paper as written. As the author of this article, if you were going to freely disclose your viewpoint, how would you identify yourself?

52.   Before you began to read this book you were asked to do the following exercise:

George Washington said, "Government is not reason; it is not eloquence, it is force. Like fire, it is a dangerous servant and a fearful master." Do you see government as a necessary good or a necessary evil? Explain your answer.

Now that you have finished this book, would you alter your answer in any way to the above question, and if so, why? If not, why?

Answers

Uncle Eric's Model of How the World Works

Short Answer/Fill-in/True or False

1. Uncle Eric says that models are how we think. They are how we understand how the world works.

2. According to Uncle Eric, models are important because we constantly refer to our models to help us determine what incoming data is important and what data is not.

3. It is important to sort incoming data because we need to decide what incoming data we need to remember or file for future reference, and what data we can discard, based on its importance to us, or its usefulness. We need a tool for making this determination. That tool is also called our "model."

4. This answer requires the student to draw his/her own conclusion based on the information provided in the explanation of "Uncle Eric's Model of How the World Works." Possible answer: We should always be willing to test our models against incoming data, and if our models don't stand up to the incoming data, then it becomes necessary to question and perhaps rethink our model, as well as question the reliability of the incoming data.

5. Free market economics and Higher Law are the two models Uncle Eric thinks are most reliable, as well as crucially important for everyone to learn. Free market economics and Higher Law are important models because they show how human civilization works, especially the world of money.

6. **Fascism** is the political philosophy that is no philosophy at all. It embraces the concept that those in power can do whatever appears necessary to achieve their goals.

Discussion/Essay/Assignment

7. Examples of models will vary and might include scientific models, religious models, economic models, political models, etc.

8. The book ARE YOU LIBERAL? CONSERVATIVE? OR CONFUSED? explains various political philosophies and which are most consistent with free markets and Higher Law principles and which are not.

9. Answers will vary.

10. Look at the front matter of your dictionary. There should be an explanation of the "Order of Definitions." For example, the order of definitions can be historical order: the earliest meaning is placed first and later meanings are arranged by semantic development.

11. The reader must understand what the author means by the words the author uses so the reader can understand the progression of the author's ideas that build on the definition of the terms used. This does not require that a reader agree with the author's definition of a word, only that the reader understand what the author means when the author uses the word. Then the reader is in a better position to critically examine the author's ideas based on a common understanding of the author's meaning.

12. Answers will vary, but might include some of the following explanations: Definitions provide clear understanding and communication between the parties involved. For example, suppose you eat a piece of

fruit. This fruit happens to be a banana. Someone comes along who has never before seen or tasted a banana. With the banana in your presence, you can each begin to discuss its merits, and you will each know exactly what you're talking about. As in the Richard Feynman example, you are understanding the characteristics of the banana that go into making up what that "thing" is. To be able to give the "thing" a name, banana, that both parties can use in future communication will help promote speedier and clearer communication. This is the purpose of always making sure that you understand the definition of a term used in a discussion (whether in conversation or in books). You don't have to agree with the person's definition, but if you understand what the person means by it, you can have a clearer and more meaningful discussion instead of getting bogged down in misunderstandings regarding fuzzy language.

Author's Disclosure

Short Answer/Fill-in/True or False

1. Juris Naturalism is the belief in a Natural Law that is higher than any government's law.

Discussion/Essay/Assignment

2. Answers will vary, but students should note that the bias or philosophical slant of an author, news commentator, or reporter can influence the selection of facts included in a book or report, thereby slanting the history, or other subject areas.

3. Answers will vary.
4. Answers will vary.
5. Answers will vary.
6. Answers will vary.

Thought Questions

Short Answer/Fill-In/True or False

1. Answers will vary, but should be logical and show thought.

2. No, the U.S. Government has not heeded George Washington's advice to avoid as little political connection as possible with foreign nations. Examples might include current political alliances, as well as past alliances, U.S. involvement in the United Nations, and U.S. troops stationed in foreign countries.

3. The United Nations came into being on June 26, 1945, and included representatives from 50 nations committing themselves to avoid war and settle disputes via negotiation and compromise. In 2003, the United Nations consisted of 191 member states.

4. Businesses, churches, charities, and other private institutions use persuasion to convince consumers to buy what they are selling or participate in their programs.

5. Government has the right to use legal force to make people do what government wants them to do.

Before beginning this book

If the Founders themselves studied ancient and modern civilizations to discover what worked and what did not in their efforts to structure a government that would provide its citizens the greatest economic prosperity and greatest degree of liberty, then ask yourself if the individual to whom you are talking has done a similar amount of research and thinking regarding this topic as did America's Founders.

Chapter 1: Don't Be Embarrassed

Thought Questions

1. Answer will vary.

2. Answers will vary.

3. Answers will vary.

Define

J. 4. Liberal. A person on the left side of the left-right political spectrum. Believes in social freedom and economic control.

D. 5. Conservative. A person on the right side of the left-right political spectrum. Believes in economic freedom and social control.

I. 6. Left. The liberal side of the political spectrum.

O. 7. Right. The conservative side of the political spectrum.

E. 8. Democrat. A person on the left side of the political spectrum.

N. 9. Republican. A person on the right side of the political spectrum.

L. 10. Moderate. One who is in the middle of the left-right political spectrum. Advocates both economic encroachment and social encroachment, but perhaps not to the extremes that left and right do.

P. 11. Socialist. A person who advocates socialism. Most have good intentions, they assume government agencies will act in the best interests of the governed, not in the best interests of the government. A Marxist.

C. 12. Communist. Originally, a Socialist who is striving for the utopia of communism in which there is no government and all live according to the rule, "from each according to his ability, to each according to his needs." Now, one who believes in a dictatorial government that owns and controls everything and everyone.

G. 13. Fascist. One who believes there is no real truth and that concepts such as justice and right and wrong are entirely matters of opinion. Also considered nationalists who believe in strong central government that controls everyone according to the rule, "do whatever appears necessary." Often intolerant of minorities.

K. 14. Libertarian. Classical Liberal.

A. 15. Centrist. Moderate.

M. 16. Populist. One who is not a Democrat or Republican but claims to be popular with rank and file voters.

B. 17. Common law. The system for discovering and applying the Natural Laws that determine the results of human behavior. The system for discovering and applying the Natural Laws that govern the human ecology. The body of definitions and precedents growing from the two fundamental laws that make civilization possible: (1) Do all you have agreed to do, and (2) do not encroach on other persons or their property.

H. 18. Hard Science. A science in which facts are mathematically measurable and provable through experimentation and observation. Examples: Physics, chemistry, biology, astronomy.

F. 19. Editorial. A statement of opinion.

Short Answer/Fill-In/True or False

20. American courts use defense attorneys as well as prosecuting attorneys because our courts are based on old English common law, which says that truth is best discovered by listening to a debate between advocates.

21. True objectivity is unlikely for a writer because a writer is usually subject to space restraints and must make choices as to what information to include and what information to omit. The choice on what to omit is based on the author's view of how the world works, and this is subjective opinion. To appear objective the writer resorts to the left-right political spectrum.

22. Resorting to the left/right political spectrum is wrong on three points: 1) the range of viewpoints is much greater than left and right. 2) The writer is usually more skilled at presenting his own opinion than the opinion of others. 3) The use of left/right has led to oversimplification.

23. Uncle Eric tries to avoid the objectivity trap by freely disclosing his viewpoint so readers can search for opposing viewpoints if they so choose.

24. At the end of Chapter One, Uncle Eric refers to his viewpoint as "the original American philosophy found in the original writings of America's Founders."

Discussion/Essay/Assignment

25. Edited "controversial topic" paper should be reduced by 50%.
26. Answers will vary. Save the list.

Chapter 2: The Original American Philosophy

Define

B. 1. Classical Liberal. Juris Naturalist. One who believes that the country should have a small, weak government, and free markets, and that the individual is endowed by his Creator with inalienable rights to his life, liberty, and property. Also, one who believes in Natural Law and common law, or Higher Law.

A. 2. Civil Libertarian. One who believes strongly in the need to protect the individual's rights to free speech, press, religion, assembly, and privacy, but usually not property.

H. 3. Juris Naturalis. Natural Law.

L. 4. Natural Law. The rules that govern the operation of the universe and everything and everyone in it.

G. 5. Higher Law. A law higher than any human law.

K. 6. Law. Broadly speaking, the rules for human conduct which are enforced by violence or threats of violence. More narrowly, law sometimes means common law or Natural Law, as distinct from legislation. "A nation of laws and not of men" means a nation in which the highest law is common law or Natural Law, not legislation.

C. 7. Contract law. Law of agreements.

E. 8. Encroach. To intrude on, or damage, the life, liberty, or property of someone who has not harmed anyone. To trespass.

O. 9. Tort law. The branch of common law dealing with harm one person does to another.

D. 10. Criminal law. Laws enacted by governments. Usually taken to mean laws against violence, fraud, and theft, but, in actual fact, governments tend to criminalize anything they don't like.

J. 11. Juris Naturalist. syn. Classical Liberal. Believes in Higher Law or Natural Law, that right and wrong are not matters of opinion. Believes political power corrupts both morals and judgment. Wants a government that is small and growing smaller.

I. 12. Juris Naturalism. The belief that there is a Natural Law that determines the results of human conduct and this law is higher than any government's law.

M. 13. Political power. The legal privilege of encroaching on the life, liberty, or property of a person who has not harmed anyone.

F. 14. Government. An organization with the legal privilege of encroaching on persons who have not harmed anyone.

N. 15. State. Government. Also sometimes means the combination of the government and the country as a single entity.

Short Answer/Fill-In/True or False

16. Classical Liberalism is the political viewpoint that represents the philosophy of America's Founders.

17. Uncle Eric advises that a person always define terms in order to avoid miscommunication and misunderstanding.

18. Higher Law is above any government's law.

19. True. Higher Law is the belief that right and wrong are not matters of opinion.

20. False. Higher Law cannot be made up by human beings. It already exists, like the laws of science, only to be discovered by humans.

21. When governments violate Higher Law, life for most of society gets worse.

22. According to Uncle Eric, the two laws that are common to all major religions and philosophies are: 1) do all you have agreed to do, and 2) do not encroach on other persons or their property.

23. The origin of the American system of liberty was **common** law.

24. Yes, according to America's Founders, government should be subject to the same principles of Higher Law as individual citizens.

25. A fundamental principle of Higher Law is that a government cannot make up laws of human conduct any more than it can make up laws of hard sciences (physics, chemistry).

26. No, government and law are not the same thing.

27. The Juris Naturalist believes government will exist, and that is why America's Founders tried to design a system of government that would restrain the growth of government.

28. The Juris Naturalist believes the most important question for public debate is, "How can we get this or that essential service without it being done by government?"

29. According to the Juris Naturalist, government should be used to solve problems only in cases where the benefits are greater than the costs.

Discussion/Essay/Assignment

30. Answers will vary but should show logic and thought.

31. Answers will vary.

32. Answers will vary, but might include: eminent domain, taxation, military draft.

33. Answers will vary but should show logic and thought.

Chapter 3: The Opposite of the Original American Philosophy

Define

1. Statist. One who believes in government as the solution to problems. Statists assume the benefits of government activities can be greater than total costs.

Short Answer/Fill-In/True or False

2. True. A statist believes government can perform services in which benefits are greater than total costs.

Discussion/Essay/Assignment

3. Answers will vary. Examples: prescription drug, health care, pollution, the economy, etc.

4. Answers will vary.

5. Subsidies are hidden taxes (suggested bills: water, phone, electric, natural gas, gasoline)

Chapter 4: Basic Political Spectrum

Short Answer/Fill-In

1. Democrats sit on the left side; Republicans sit on the right.

2. Liberals emphasize caring, gentleness, and progress.

3. Conservatives emphasize ruggedness, endurance, and stability.

4. Liberals are doves; Conservatives are hawks.

Discussion/Essay/Assignment

5. Answers will vary but should show logic and thought.

Chapter 5: The Nature of Political Power

Define

1. Influence. Persuasion. Implies the ability to say no without being punished.

Short Answer/Fill-In/True or False

2. Answers may vary, but Uncle Eric can think of no one other than government that can legally use brute force on its customers/citizens.

3. America's Founders tried to protect individual citizens from government's political power by establishing a government restricted by a system of checks and balances, a system of law based on Higher Law principles to which both individual citizens as well as government servants were required to adhere, term limits, recall and impeachment, veto, court review, and other restraints.

4. Political power permits the use of brute force. Influence implies choice.

5. If you do not comply with certain political laws you can be taken away by brute force or your property can be confiscated. Examples of these political laws may include: military conscription, drugs, gun ownership, income taxes, Social Security tax, property tax.

For Research

6. Answers will vary.
7. Answers will vary.

Chapter 6: The Two Categories of Encroachment

Define

1. Wealth. Goods and services. Not to be confused with money. Money can be wealth, but it is only one kind.

Short Answer/Fill-In/True or False

2. Juris Naturalists attempt to solve the problems of poverty, drug addiction, education of children, etc. through non-government means. The Juris Naturalist prefers private and voluntary solutions.

Discussion/Essay/Assignment

3. Answers will vary. Does the research support or negate Uncle Eric's conclusion "that liberals are Juris Naturalists in social matters, but they tend to be statists in economic matters, and Conservatives tend to be Juris Naturalists in economic matters and statists in social matters"?

4. Research results will vary.

5. Research papers will vary. Look for thoroughness and sources consulted for research.

Chapter 7: The Middle Ground

Short Answer/Fill-In/True or False

1. Another name for Moderate is Centrist.

2. Moderates are in the center of what are considered the extreme positions of the Liberal and Conservative positions.

3. Moderates want to control a person's economic and social conduct.

4. Moderates don't like privacy because they want to monitor all conduct, both economic and social.

5. False. Correct statement: The total amount of power a Moderate wishes to hold over another person is equal to or greater than that desired by either left or right because the Moderate wants to control both a person's economic and social conduct.

Chapter 8: Freedom vs. Liberty

Define

1. Freedom. Permission to do as you please.

2. Liberty. Protection of the individual's rights to his or her life, liberty, and property. Widespread obedience to the two fundamental laws that make civilization possible: (1) do all you have agreed to do, and (2) do not encroach on other persons or their property. Liberty is not the same as freedom.

Short Answer/Fill-In/True or False

3. When an individual encroaches on someone else, that individual has made a decision to place him/her self outside the laws of civilization — becoming an outlaw, no longer protected by the laws of liberty.

Discussion/Essay/Assignment

4. Answers will vary, but some suggestions are: Jesse James, Black Bart, the Dalton Gang, Butch Cassidy, the Sundance Kid, Billy the Kid.

5. Answers will vary.

6. Answers will vary.

7. America's Founders were fighting for liberty, not democracy. They wanted a government that would be constrained by Higher Law principles; in a democracy, the majority could steer the course of conduct, whether the majority's choices in law was right or wrong. Examples: slavery in America or Japanese internment during WWII.

8. Answers will vary, but it should be noted that democracies are based on majority rule whether the rule is right or wrong; a republic founded on common law/Natural Law/Higher Law is restrained by those laws.

Chapter 9: Exceptions

Define

1. Socialism. An economic and political system under which virtually everything and everyone is owned and controlled by government agencies. Marxism.

Short Answer/Fill-In/True or False

2. Liberty is usually lost by people allowing exceptions into law that destroy the liberty on which the country was originally founded.

Discussion/Essay/Assignment

3-7. Answers will vary.

Chapter 10: Military and Foreign Policy

Short Answer/Fill-In/True or False

1. Until the collapse of the Soviet Empire, Liberals did not want officials to form military alliances or intervene in the political affairs of other nations. They made an exception in the area of economic assistance. They were willing to raise taxes at home to finance aid to the poor abroad.

2. Prior to the collapse of the former Soviet Empire, Conservatives were willing to form military alliances with other nations whose officials claimed to be anti-Soviet. They were also willing to intervene in the affairs of foreign nations to keep them from drifting toward the left. They did not want to send money to the poor of foreign nations.

3. The Juris Naturalist says we should never interfere or intervene in the politics of other countries; we cannot begin to understand them. The result will inevitably draw us into war.

4. Some wars from the 20th century in which the U.S. participated include World War I, World War II, Korea, Vietnam, and the Iraq-Kuwait War.

5. The Bill of Rights protects people from the U.S. Government's misbehavior towards individuals within the borders of the United States, but it does not provide protections from U.S. Government misbehavior outside the borders of the United States.

6. The isolationist wants nothing to do with foreign nations. Individuals who believe in political neutrality do not want to get involved in the political affairs of foreign nations, but they do want to visit and trade with them.

7. No, George Washington believed in political neutrality.

Discussion/Essay/Assignment

8-10. Answers will vary.

11. This will require research and the answer will be subject to change as alliances change. In his FAREWELL ADDRESS George Washington cautioned against forming political alliances with other countries.

12. Answers will vary.

Chapter 11: Democrats and Republicans

Define

1. Democrat. Liberal.

2. Republican. Conservative.

3. Capitalist. One who believes in capitalism.

4. Capitalism. A term coined by Socialist Karl Marx, who meant the stage of economic development in which large amounts of capital (tools) are accumulated by private firms. Today capitalism is generally taken to mean free markets, free trade, and free enterprise. The economic philosophy of the right/Conservatives.

Short Answer/Fill-In/True or False

5. In the U.S. the party of the left is the Democrats.

6. In the U.S. the party of the right is the Republicans.

7. Both Democrats and Republicans tend to hover close to the center of the political spectrum because that's where most of the voters tend to be.

8. Yes, this tendency to hover close to center makes it difficult to differentiate candidates from the two parties.

9. Another word for free markets is capitalism.

10. One type of capitalist believes in capitalism; the other type of capitalist participates in capitalism but does not believe in capitalism.

11. The result of the capitalist who says he/she believes in capitalism but doesn't follow the philosophy is that this type of capitalist, in efforts to reduce competition and increase profit, will go to government to seek subsidies, entitlements, privileges, handouts, etc.

Discussion/Essay/Assignment

12. Answers will vary
13. Answers will vary
14. Answers will vary, but Uncle Eric would be in agreement with each quoted sentiment.

Chapter 12: Socialism and Communism

Define

1. Liberalism. The philosophy of the left. Borrows much from socialism. Believes in economic statism, freedom in most non-economic matters, and less militarism.

2. Socialist. A person who advocates socialism. Most Socialists have good intentions, they assume government agencies will act in the best interests of the governed, not in the best interests of the government. A Marxist.

3. Marxism. The theory of Karl Marx is that human society develops through stages ending in a utopia called communism. It is the belief that a dictatorial government that owns and controls everything and everyone (socialism) is a necessary step on the road to communism.

4. Marxist. One who believes in the economic philosophy of Karl Marx. A Socialist or Communist.

5. Welfare statism. The belief that government should ensure a minimum standard of living for all, which includes, but is not necessarily limited to, food, clothing, shelter, medical care, and schooling. Requires heavy taxes and a large bureaucracy to finance and administer the welfare programs. Probably the most popular leftist economic philosophy.

Short Answer/Fill-In/True or False

6. A Socialist is someone who wants vast power over our economic affairs so that inequality of wealth can be greatly reduced and poverty eliminated.

7. Communism is assumed to be a ruthless police state little different than Nazi Germany. The former Soviet Union, Red China, and Cuba are examples of the communist economic system.

8. True. The early American colonies were founded on the system of mercantilism.

9. Welfare statism is the most common form of socialism found in the U.S. today.

10. Welfare statism programs in the U.S. today include: Social Security, Medicare, Aid to Families with Dependent Children.

11. America began to implement socialist programs in the 1930s.

12. The Great Depression in the 1930s was the event that caused U.S. citizens to look to government to take care of citizens.

Discussion/Essay/Assignment

13. The six stages of dialectical materialism are:

    1. Primitive slave state. No freedom, no free trade, and the government controls everything for the good of the government. People are property with no rights. Life is short and filled with disease, hunger, and filth.

    2. Feudalism. Small independent kingdoms insulated from the rest of the world. Little free trade. The king or feudal lord controls the land within the kingdom, forms alliances with other lords and kings, and controls the impoverished workers — the serfs — and taxes them heavily. Life is short and filled with disease, hunger, and filth.

    3. Mercantilism. Large nations with large governments. Rulers believe money is wealth. They arrange for goods to be exported so that money can be imported to fill the government's reserves. Enormous wars erupt. Taxes are heavy, and there is some free trade. The government has minor respect for an individual's rights to life, liberty and property. Life is short and filled with disease, hunger and filth.

    4. Capitalism. Great emphasis on free trade and limited government. Belief in an individual's rights to his life, liberty, and property. Massive amounts of savings accumulate because of low taxes — these savings are available to create sources for jobs and production. Life spans are longer because disease, filth and hunger are much less.

    5. Socialism. No free trade and no personal freedom. All people and material objects are owned by the government for the "good of society." The purpose of socialism is to prepare the way for communism. The nations of the former Soviet Empire were tests for various degrees of socialism. They were all unsuccessful.

6. Communism. The utopian stage of socialism in which government disappears and individuals live under the rule, "from each according to his ability, to each according to his need." All the products and benefits from labor are contributed to a common pool from which each person takes what he/she needs. Communism is an ideal in which there is no government.

14. Some examples of socialist programs in the U.S. include: Social Security, medicare, Aid to Families with Dependent Children (research to find other programs, or listen to forthcoming promises of aid from campaigning politicians).

15. One explanation that is different from Uncle Eric's is that the people, although concerned about the Social Security program, were told it was an insurance program. Like home, auto, medical insurance, they believed they were funding a program that would be self-supporting, as is private insurance. So, rather than looking for a handout, they believed they were buying another type of insurance.

Chapter 13: Fascism

Define

1. Fascism. The political philosophy that is no philosophy at all, do whatever appears necessary. Derived from the law of the Roman Empire.

2. Fascist. One who believes there is no real truth. The true fascist believes that concepts such as justice, and right and wrong are entirely matters of opinion. Fascists are nationalists who believe in strong central government that controls everyone according to the rule, "do whatever appears necessary." Often fascists are intolerant of minorities.

Short Answer/Fill-In/True or False

3. Fascism is unique among the "isms" because it has no intellectual leadership.

4. Answers:

    John Maynard Keynes: welfare statists

    Adam Smith: Conservatives

    Karl Marx: Socialists

    America's Founders: Juris Naturalists

    No intellectual leader: Fascists

5. The basic premise of fascism is that all truth is a matter of opinion; what counts is action. Might makes right.

6. Fascist leaders include: Adolf Hitler, Mussolini, Franco, Tojo.

7. Pragmatism, as it relates to fascists, means that powerholders should do anything that appears necessary, with no moral limits, to achieve their objectives. The end justifies the means.

8. Uncle Eric means that fascists will temporarily adopt whatever philosophy is necessary to achieve their ends. If capitalism is necessary they will embrace capitalism, but they can change their policies with no warning, leaving citizens vulnerable to the whims of the fascist: personally, economically and legally.

9. The ingredient necessary to keep a powerholder controlled is a legal system that holds powerholders, as well as every other citizen, accountable to Higher Law principles.

Discussion/Essay/Assignment

10. Opinions may vary, however, internment of the Japanese-Americans was a violation of their rights as no evidence was provided for incarceration.

11. Answers will vary, however, without a system of Higher Law to keep the exercise of political power restrained, government will grow excessively as will government's exercise of power.

12. Answers will vary

For Research

13. Answers will vary.

Chapter 14: What Are They Really?

For Research/Discussion

1-2. Answers will vary.

Chapter 15: The Other Middle View

Short Answer/Fill-In/True or False

1. Moderates combine the left's desire to encroach on economic affairs and the right's desire to encroach on social affairs.

2. Juris Naturalists combine the left's desire for liberty in social affairs and the right's desire for liberty in economic affairs.

3. Juris Naturalists are terrified of **political power.**

4. Prior to the 20th century, the Federal government was financed entirely through liquor, tobacco, and import taxes. There was no federal income tax.

For Research/Discussion

5-6. Research project. Answers will vary.

Chapter 16: The National Religion

Short Answer/Fill-In/True or False

1. The Juris Naturalist prefers to find a voluntary private solution to problems rather than political/governmental solutions.

2. Uncle Eric believes the root cause of poverty, business failures, and unemployment are problems of character.

3. Uncle Eric believes the only real solution to our country's problems is to get back to the fundamental principles that lead to strong character.

Discussion/Essay/Assignment

4. Answers will vary.

5. Answers will vary. Possible examples: "Little House on the Prairie" television series, "Dr. Quinn, Medicine Woman" television series.

6. Possible answer: The Amish communities rely on themselves to solve their problems.

7. Answers will vary based on the time period in which this question is being answered.

8. Answers will vary. Suggested: The expression "doing business on a handshake" means the person's character is strong enough to seal the deal - no attorneys are needed, no written contract, just the individuals' promise to execute the verbal agreement. This type of business is most likely to be practiced, if at all, in small towns where reputations of individuals are known. By contrast, the chance of doing business on a handshake in today's world is limited.

Chapter 17: A U.S.-Nazi Alliance or a U.S.-Soviet Alliance?

Short Answer/Fill-In/True or False

1. Answer: Left = socialism/Stalin; Right = fascism/Hitler; Juris Naturalist = political neutrality/America's Founders

2. During World War II, America's political leaders allied themselves with Stalin who embraced socialism.

3. The leftist view was most popular in America because of the perceived success of Franklin Roosevelt's New Deal.

4. The isolationist wants nothing to do with any other country. However, a person who believes in political neutrality wants to travel to other countries, do business with other countries, make friends in other countries – he/she just doesn't want to form political connections of any kind with other countries.

Discussion/Essay/Assignment:

5. Answers will vary.

Chapter 18: Economic Counterparts

Define

1. Keynesianism. Originally the economic philosophy of economist John Maynard Keynes. Today a kind of compromise, or middle road, between socialism and capitalism. Wants broad government controls on economic activity, especially manipulation of the money supply. "Keynesian" is sometimes used as a synonym for "inflationist," or one who advocates inflating the money supply.

2. Monetarism. A free-market economic philosophy. Sometimes called the Chicago School of Economics (associated with the economics department of the University of Chicago). Focuses on increases in money supply, causing rising prices.

3. Austrian Economics. The most free-market of all the economic viewpoints today. The origin was in Vienna, Austria, but the country where it is most popular today is probably the U.S. Austrian economists have won Nobel Prizes, and the most widely known Austrian economist, F.H. Hayek, was highly influential in the economic policies of British Prime Minister Margaret Thatcher.

4. Laissez faire capitalism. From the French, laissez nous faire, meaning leave us alone. Says the benefits of government's economic controls are less than the total costs. Government should do nothing in the economy except enforce contracts and protect against violence and theft.

Short Answer/Fill-In/True or False

5. In 1913 the federal income tax was created through the 16th amendment to the Constitution (research will be required to discover this answer).

6. The Federal government, prior to income tax, received almost 100% of its tax revenue from liquor, tobacco, and import taxes.

7. In 1995 taxes from liquor, tobacco, and imports accounted for about 3% of the Federal government's receipts. The balance of the Federal government's receipts come from taxes created beyond what America's Founders originally created.

8. True. Government spends much of its time redistributing the money it collects which causes economic philosophy to be a huge part of political philosophy.

9. The economics of the far left is called socialism or Marxism.

10. The economics of the center-left is called Keynesianism, a compromise socialism.

11. The economics of the right is called monetarism.

12. The economics of the extreme right is called fascism.

13. The economics of the Juris Naturalist is called Austrian economics or laissez faire capitalism.

14. The dominant economic policy during America's first 150 years was laissez faire capitalism.

Discussion/Essay/Assignment

15. Answers will vary.

Chapter 19: Effects on Your Money

Define

1. Communist. Originally, a Socialist who is striving for the utopia of communism in which there is no government and all live according to the rule, "from each according to his ability, to each according to his needs." Now, one who believes in a dictatorial government that owns and controls everything and everyone.

Short Answer/Fill-In/True or False

2. Liberals are more interested in good intentions than good results, according to Uncle Eric. Liberals are more willing to enact higher taxes and initiate more controls to fight poverty.

3. Liberals see business as predatory and business income as a source of potential revenue for liberal programs.

4. The potential repercussions to employees whose employers have been taxed by liberal programs are that employees might find themselves out of a job if the employer goes out of business due to new controls or taxes.

5. Leftist monetary policy can affect investment markets by causing wild swings in interest rates and in stock and bond values.

6. Conservatives want to use government policy to control behavior, and these controls result in a decrease in personal privacy. Conservatives are more likely to want to go to war to stop threats against America, which means higher taxes to fight war.

7. Uncle Eric says liberal policies lead to higher taxes and conservative policies lead to a reduction of personal liberty.

8. As long as people keep their agreements and don't encroach on each other or each other's property, the Juris Naturalist does not want to use the force of law on a person.

Discussion/Essay/Assignment

9-13. Answers will vary.

Chapter 20: Three Types of Wrongdoing

Define

1. Manners. Polite behavior. Courteous deportment.

2. Tort. Harm done to another. Encroachment on the life, liberty, or property of a person who has not harmed anyone.

Short Answer/Fill-In/True or False

3. Tort, which is harm done to others through the use of fraud, theft, or force is serious enough to warrant intervention by law.

4. The most important idea separating Juris Naturalists from others is that in public policy matters the Juris Naturalist is concerned only about torts, while others will use legislation to try to control behaviors that are not torts.

Chapter 21: Muddied Waters

Define

1. Anarchism. Originally, advocating no political government. Now often used to mean advocating terrorism.

2. Terrorism. The creation of terror, usually through violence or threats of violence. As commonly used, automatically assumes the terrorist is acting without good cause.

3. Politicize. To make political. To be entangled in the struggle for political power. To be under the government's control.

4. Warlord. Originally, a high-ranking military officer in charge of a medieval kingdom's military operations. Now, an enemy military leader.

5. Populist. One who is not a Democrat or Republican but claims to be popular with rank and file voters.

6. Bolshevik. Originally, a member of the Social Democratic Party of Russia around 1917. Now, any Socialist or Communist.

7. Nationalist. An extremely patriotic person who regards his nation as being of supreme importance.

8. Civil Libertarian. One who believes strongly in the need to protect the individual's rights to free speech, press, religion, assembly, and privacy, but usually not property.

9. Radical, Extremist, Fanatic. One who is highly committed to a cause with which the writer or speaker does not agree.

Short Answer/Fill-In/True or False

10. Uncle Eric advises that the reader or listener always try to learn the belief or definition of words being used by a writer, lecturer, teacher, media commentator, etc. Never assume you know how a speaker or author is using terminology that has not been clearly defined by that speaker or writer.

Chapter 22: Who Gets the Children?

Discussion/Essay/Assignment

1. Answers will vary.

Chapter 23: The Return of Racism

Discussion/Essay/Assignment

1-2. Answers will vary.

Chapter 24: The First American Philosophies

Short Answer/Fill-In/True or False

1. Henry and Madison were on opposite sides of the constitutional debate (Madison was a Federalist and Henry was an anti-Federalist) but both turned out to be right in their economic predictions.

2. Madison wanted a federal government so it could control state governments. He feared state democracies would evolve into dictatorships of the majority over the minority that would grow to tax and control every aspect of American life. Madison feared unemployment and widespread business failure if the power of the states continued to expand. Henry felt another layer of government (federal in addition to the state government) would "oppress and ruin" people. He predicted a giant bureaucracy and military empire that would tax and harass people at home, as well as get Americans involved in wars abroad.

3. Both Madison and Henry were afraid of political power and both were trying to invent a system of government that would minimize political power.

Discussion/Essay/Assignment

4-6. Answers will vary.

7. Answers will vary, but student should note that it was intended that the Federal government only be permitted to exercise powers given to it by the Constitution and not prohibited by the States or the people.

Chapter 25: Summary

Short Answer/Fill-In

1. In order to understand political philosophies, one should focus attention on liberty versus political power.

2. Liberals, Moderates, and Conservatives all compete for political power.

3. The Juris Naturalist wants to minimize political power and increase individual liberty.

4. According to Uncle Eric, Liberals, Moderates, and Conservatives are all statists.

5. Liberals want to control your economic conduct.

6. Conservatives want to control your social conduct.

7. Moderates want to control both your economic and social conduct.

8. Juris Naturalists only want to control conduct that is consistent with the two fundamental laws that make civilization possible.

9. The two fundamental laws that make civilization possible are: 1) do all you have agreed to do, and 2) do not encroach on other persons or their property.

10. America's Founders embraced the political philosophy that Uncle Eric now calls Juris Naturalism.

11. The writer slants his work based on the facts he chooses to report. Due to space limitations a writer finds it impossible to report all viewpoints and all facts. By necessity of space or time the writer must make choices about what will be included and what will be omitted. The writer chooses what the writer determines is important and omits the rest.

Discussion/Essay/Assignment

12-13. Answers will vary.

For Research

14. Answers will vary.

Chapter 26: Encroachment: Big and Small

Discussion/Essay/Assignment

1. Answers will vary.

Final Exam Answers

1. Liberal. A person on the left side of the left-right political spectrum. Liberals believe in social freedom and economic control.

2. Conservative. A person on the right side of the left-right political spectrum. Conservatives believe in economic freedom and social control.

3. True. A Democrat is a person on the left side of the political spectrum.

4. True. A Republican is a person on the right side of the political spectrum

5. Socialist. A person who advocates socialism. Most Socialists have good intentions; they assume government agencies will act in the best interests of the governed, not in the best interests of the government. A Marxist.

6. Common law. The system for discovering and applying the Natural Laws that determine the results of human behavior. The system for discovering and applying the Natural Laws that govern the human ecology. The body of definitions and precedents growing from the two fundamental laws that make civilization possible: (1) do all you have agreed to do, and (2) do not encroach on other persons or their property.

7. Resorting to the left/right political spectrum is wrong on three points: 1) The range of viewpoints is much greater than left and right. 2) The writer is usually more skilled at presenting his own opinion than the opinion of others. 3) The use of left/right has led to oversimplification.

8. Classical Liberal. Juris Naturalist. One who believes that the country should have a small, weak government, and free markets, and that the individual is endowed by his Creator with inalienable rights to his life, liberty, and property. Also, one who believes in Natural law and common law, or Higher Law.

9. Juris Naturalism. The belief that there is a Natural Law that determines the results of human conduct and this law is higher than any government's law.

10. Political Power. The legal privilege of encroaching on the life, liberty, or property of a person who has not harmed anyone.

11. Higher Law is above any government's law.

12. False. Higher Law cannot be made up by human beings. It already exists, like the laws of science, and can only be *discovered* by humans.

13. According to Uncle Eric, the two laws that are common to all major religions and philosophies are: 1) do all you have agreed to do, and 2) Do not encroach on other persons or their property.

14. The Juris Naturalist believes the most important question for public debate is, "How can we get this or that essential service without it being done by government.?"

15. According to the Juris Naturalist, government should be used to solve problems only in cases where the benefits are greater than the costs.

16. True. A statist believes government can perform services in which benefits are greater than total costs.

17. Political power permits the use of brute force. Influence implies choice.

18. The Juris Naturalist attempt to solve the problems of poverty, drug addiction, education of children, etc., through non-government means; the Juris Naturalist prefers private and voluntary solutions.

19. False. Correct statement: The total amount of power a Moderate wishes to hold over another person is equal to or **greater** than that desired by either left or right because the Moderate wants to control both a person's economic and social conduct.

20. When an individual encroaches on someone else, that person has made a decision to place him/her self outside the laws of civilization - becoming an outlaw, no longer protected by the laws of liberty.

21. Freedom. Permission to do as you please.

22. Liberty. Protection of the individual's rights to his or her life, liberty, and property. Widespread obedience to the two fundamental laws that make civilization possible: 1) do all you have agreed to do, and 2) do not encroach on other persons or their property. Liberty is not the same as freedom.

23. Liberty is usually lost by people allowing exceptions into law that destroy the liberty on which the country was originally founded.

24. Regarding foreign intervention, the Juris Naturalist says we should never interfere or intervene in the politics of other countries. We cannot begin to understand them. The result will inevitably be to draw us into war.

25. The isolationist wants nothing to do with foreign nations. Individuals who believe in political neutrality do not want to get involved in the political affairs of foreign nations, but do want to visit and trade with them.

26. One type of capitalist believes in capitalism; the other type of capitalist participates in capitalism but does not believe in capitalism.

27. The result of the capitalist who says he/she believes in capitalism but doesn't follow the philosophy is that this type of capitalist, in efforts to reduce competition and increase profit, will go to government to seek subsidies, entitlements, privileges, handouts, etc.

28. A Socialist is someone who wants vast power over our economic affairs so that inequality of wealth can be greatly reduced and poverty eliminated.

29. Welfare statism is the most common form of socialism found in the U.S. today.

30. America began to implement socialist programs in the 1930s.

31. The Great Depression in the 1930s was the event that caused U.S. citizens to look to government to take care of citizens.

32. The six stages of dialectical materialism are: 1) primitive slave state, 2) feudalism, 3) mercantilism, 4) capitalism, 5) socialism, 6) communism.

33. Fascist. One who believes there is no real truth. The true fascist believes that concepts such as justice and right and wrong are entirely matters of opinion. Fascists are nationalists who believe in strong central government that controls everyone according to the rule, "do whatever appears necessary." Often fascists are intolerant of minorities.

34. Uncle Eric means that fascists will temporarily adopt whatever philosophy is necessary to achieve their ends. If capitalism is necessary they will embrace capitalism, but they can change their policies with no warning, leaving citizens vulnerable to the whims of the fascist — personally, economically and legally.

35. The ingredient necessary to keep a powerholder controlled is a legal system that holds powerholders, as well as every other citizen, accountable to Higher Law principles.

36. Moderates combine the left's desire to encroach on economic affairs and the right's desire to encroach on social affairs.

37. Juris Naturalists combine the left's desire for liberty in social affairs and the right's desire for liberty in economic affairs.

38. The Juris Naturalist prefers to find a voluntary private solution to problems rather than political/governmental solutions.

39. During World War II, America's political leaders allied themselves with Stalin who embraced socialism.

40. The leftist view was most popular in America because of the perceived success of Franklin Roosevelt's New Deal.

41. The isolationist wants nothing to do with any other country. However, a person who believes in political neutrality wants to travel to other countries, do business with other countries, make friends in other countries – he/she just doesn't want to form political connections of any kind with other countries.

42. Economics of the far left is called socialism or Marxism.

43. The economics of the center-left is called Keynesianism, a compromise socialism.

44. The dominant economic policy during America's first 150 years was laissez faire capitalism.

45. Conservatives want to use government policy to control behavior, and these controls result in a decrease in personal privacy. Conservatives are more likely to want to go to war to stop threats against America, which means higher taxes to fight war.

46. The most important idea separating Juris Naturalists from others is that in public policy matters the Juris Naturalist is concerned only about torts, while others will use legislation to try to control behaviors that are not torts.

47. Both James Madison and Patrick Henry were afraid of political power and both were trying to invent a system of government that would minimize political power.

48. According to Uncle Eric, Liberals, Moderates, and Conservatives are all statists.

49. Uncle Eric believes that whenever you read anything, other than math or the "hard sciences," you are reading an editorial because the writer slants his work based on the facts he chooses to report. Due to space limitations a writer finds it impossible to report all viewpoints and all facts. By necessity of space or time, the writer must make choices about what will be included and what will be omitted. The writer chooses what he/she determines is important and omits the rest.

50. Answers will vary.

51. Answers will vary.

52. Answers will vary.